LEARN TO DRAW

DISNEY

THE
LION KING

D1308010

Walter Foster
Jr.

Illustrated by the Disney Storybook Artists.
Step art by Greg Guler and Pablo Mendoza.

Published by Walter Foster Jr.,
an imprint of The Quarto Group.
26391 Crown Valley Parkway, Suite 220, Mission Viejo, CA 92691
www.QuartoKnows.com

Printed in China
10 9 8 7 6 5 4 3 2 1

FSC
www.fsc.org

MIX
Paper from
responsible sources
FSC® C016973

TABLE OF CONTENTS

 TOOLS & MATERIALS

You only need to gather a few simple art supplies before you begin. Start with a drawing pencil and an eraser. Make sure you also have a pencil sharpener and a ruler. To add color to your drawings, use markers, colored pencils, crayons, watercolors, or acrylic paint. The choice is yours!

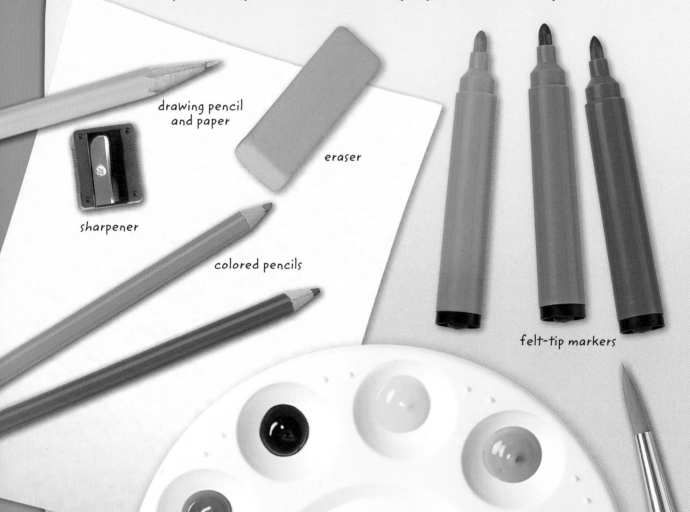

drawing pencil and paper

eraser

sharpener

colored pencils

felt-tip markers

paintbrushes and paints

HOW TO USE THIS BOOK

You can draw any of the characters in this book by following these simple steps.

◀1▶

First draw basic shapes using light lines that will be easy to erase.

◀2▶

Each new step is shown in blue, so you'll always know what to draw next.

◀3▶

Take your time and copy the blue lines, adding detail.

◀4▶

Darken the lines you want to keep and erase the rest.

◀5▶

Add color to your drawing with colored pencils, markers, paints, or crayons!

🐾 LION SYMBOL 🐾

When Prince Simba is born, King Mufasa's good friend Rafiki draws a lion cub on the baobab tree he lives in. The day Simba disappears, Rafiki, in his grief, smears the drawing. But once he realizes Simba is not dead, Rafiki exclaims, "He's alive!" and adds a mane to his drawing to represent the adult Simba.

◄1►

◄2►

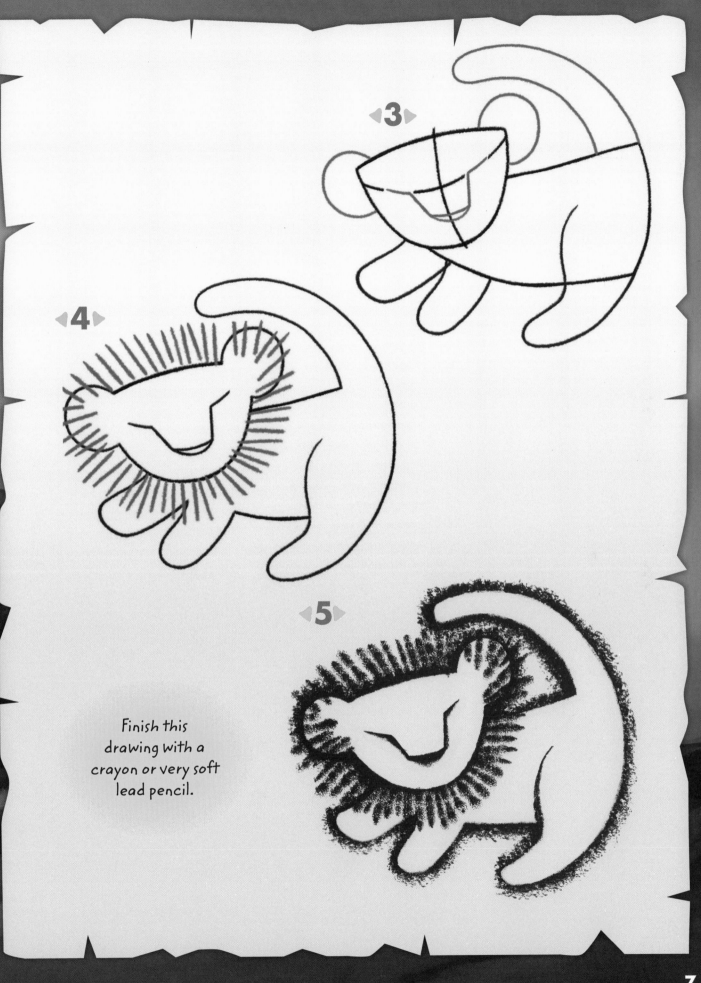

Finish this
drawing with a
crayon or very soft
lead pencil.

SIMBA

Simba can't wait to be king. But when a wildebeest stampede kills his father, King Mufasa, his evil uncle Scar blames Simba and convinces him to run away. Simba befriends Timon and Pumbaa and lives a carefree lifestyle of hakuna matata. But one day, after his old friend Nala appears and pleads with him to save the Pride Lands from Scar, Simba springs into action to take his rightful place as the Lion King.

◄3►

◄4►

◄5►

Don't forget to
draw whiskers on
Simba's muzzle.

◄6►

◄3►

Young Simba has a round, kittenish body, but he already shows signs of the king he is to become.

◄4►

◄5►

◄6►

◄7►

◄8►

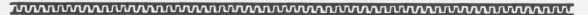

❊ NALA ❊

Simba's best friend Nala will do anything for the future king. It is Nala who finds her long-lost friend and convince him to return to the Pride Lands. After Simba finally takes the throne, Nala is at his side as the new queen.

A light tan color surrounds Nala's bright eyes, suggesting her clever, outgoing personality.

◄3►

◄4►

SCAR

Scar, the evil brother of Mufasa, wants to be king. He is witty and willing
to do anything to gain power—even if it means killing his brother
and blaming his nephew Simba. Scar becomes king of the Pride Lands,
but his rule devastates the land and endangers the pride.

4

Scar has large paws with the claws always extended.

◄5►

◄6►

7

8

TIMON

The wisecracking meerkat Timon leads the hakuna matata lifestyle of no worries, no responsibilities, and no cares. He and his warthog friend Pumbaa befriend Simba and introduce him to their philosophy. But once Simba is called into action to save the Pride Lands, both Pumbaa and Timon help restore Simba to the throne.

◀4▶

Keep Timon's body lean and his expressive face (eyes, mouth, and nose) big.

◄5►

◄6►

PUMBAA

The flatulent warthog Pumbaa is an outcast because of his foul smell. But he befriends a meerkat named Timon, and the two best friends live the carefree lifestyle of hakuna matata together. When Pumbaa and Timon stumble upon the lion cub Simba, they don't know that he's the rightful king.

◀ **5** ▶

The biggest part
of Pumbaa is
his mouth.

◀ **6** ▶

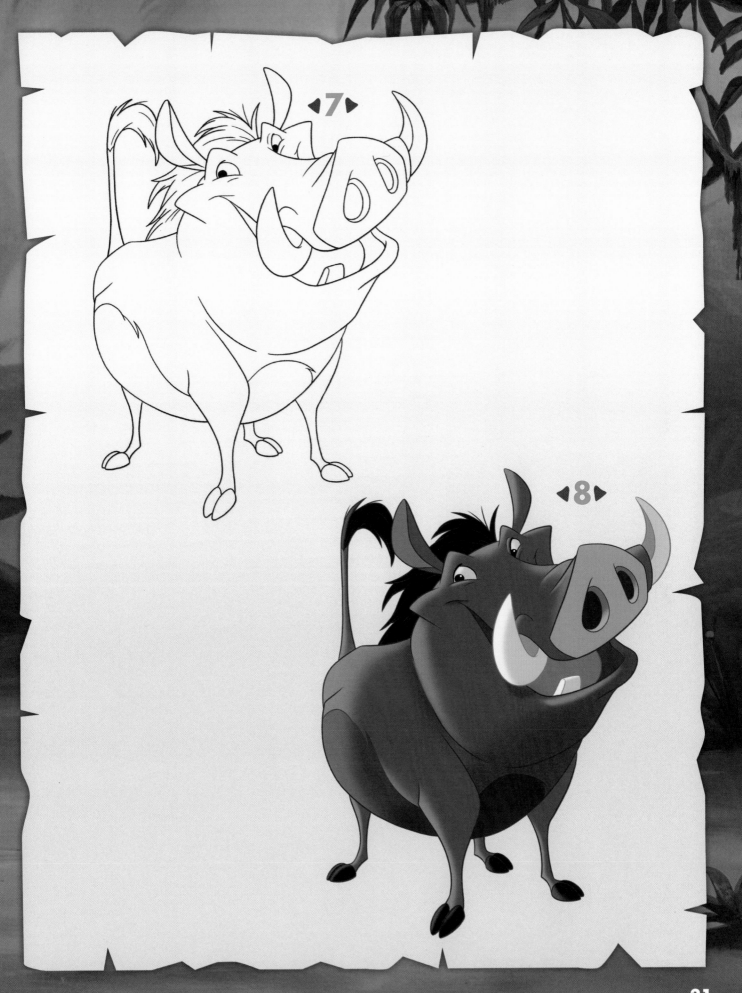

◄7►

◄8►

☀ RAFIKI ☀

Rafiki is a sage old mandrill who lives in an ancient baobab tree. This wiseman and shaman is somewhat mysterious and a little crazy, but he is a close and trusted friend of King Mufasa. When Simba needs guidance, Rafiki helps him to understand his plight and destiny.

◄1►

Rafiki's hands and feet are almost identical in size and shape. He has long limbs and a stooped body.

☀ ZAZU ☀

Zazu is a hornbill who takes his job very seriously. As Mufasa's "majordomo" or "steward," he is overzealous and overprotective as Simba's caretaker. He puts up with a lot of teasing from Simba but still watches out for the young, rambunctious lion.

◀1▶

◀2▶

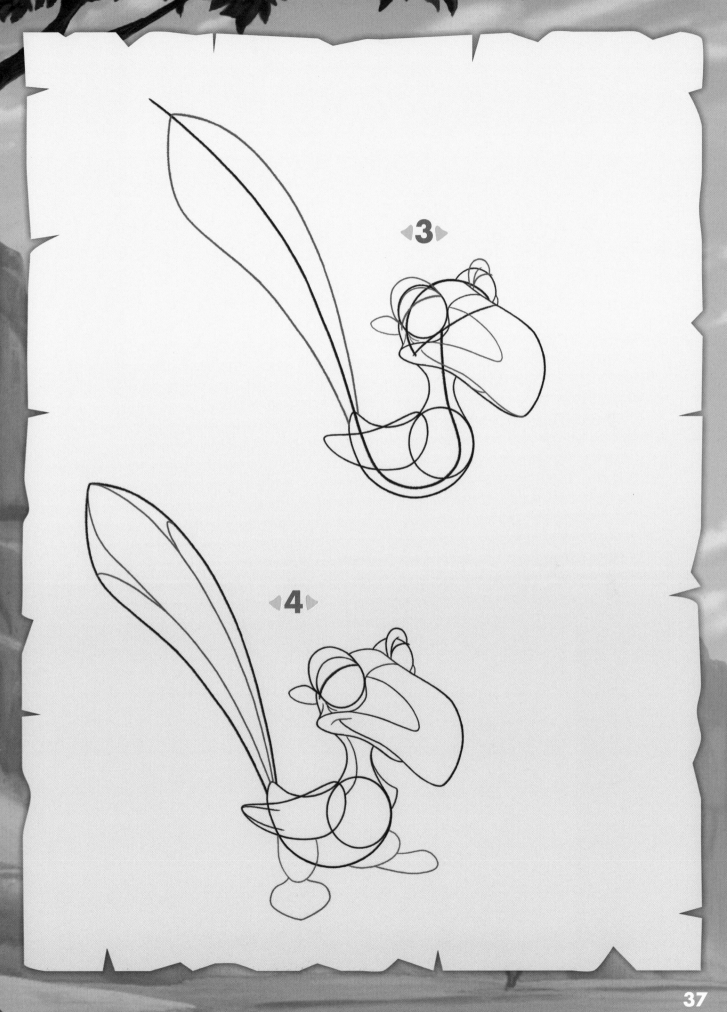

5

Zazu's triangular beak is similar in shape to his body, but larger. His long tail feathers are held straight in the air.

6

🐾 MUFASA 🐾

Mufasa is a stern but kind leader. He is a caring and nurturing father and adoring husband. He is courageous, yet cautious, and is respected by everyone except for his brother, Scar. Mufasa's jealous brother is a thorn in the king's side, but Mufasa still looks out for him, hoping that someday he will change.

◄3►

◄4►

◂5▸

◂6▸

Mufasa is bulkier than
the adult Simba. He also
has a wider muzzle and
a darker brown nose.

SARABI

Sarabi is the proud and brave Queen of Pride Rock. After losing Mufasa and her son, Simba, she's not afraid to stand up to the evil Scar, who has taken over the Pride Lands. It is her job to hunt for food for the pride, but there is no food left. She tries to convince Scar that they must leave the now-barren Pride Lands, but he refuses.

◄3►

◄4►

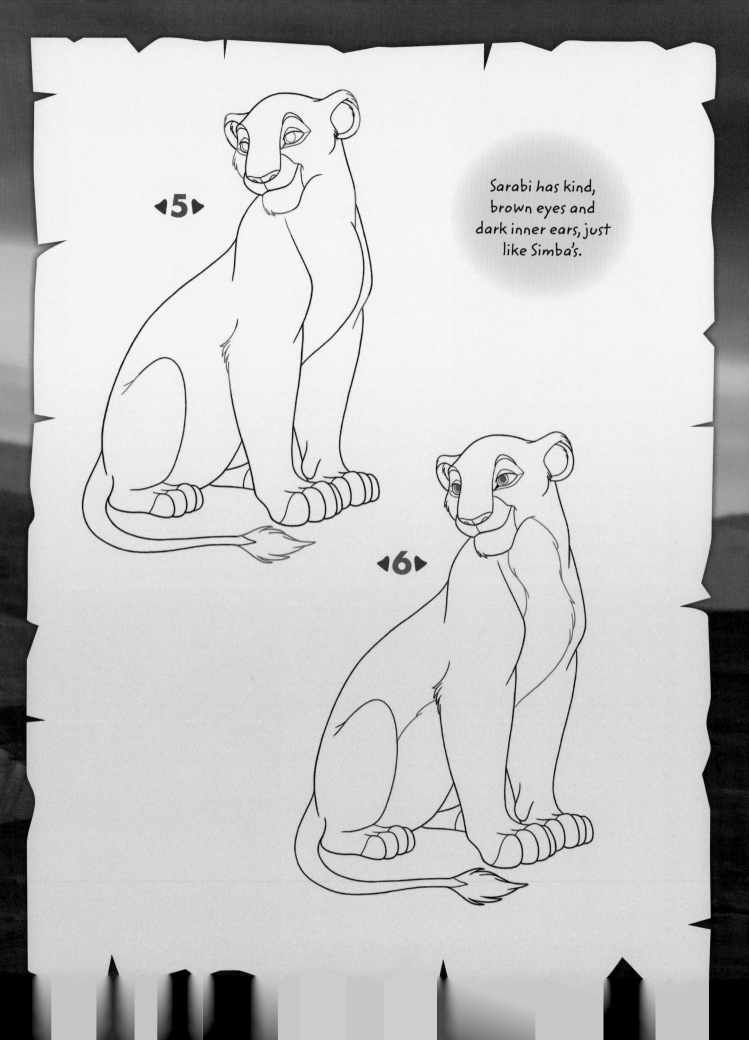

◀5▶

◀6▶

Sarabi has kind, brown eyes and dark inner ears, just like Simba's.

◀7▶

◀8▶

ADULT SIMBA

After Simba ran away, he met Timon and Pumbaa and grew up living the carefree life of hakuna matata. It is only when his old friend Nala discovers that he is alive does Simba agree to go back to take his rightful place as King of the Pride Lands.

◄1►

◄2►

Simba's eyes stay round and large, even as an adult. Show Simba's power in his broad shoulders and chest.

◄3►

◄4►

◀7▶

◀8▶

SCAR IN ACTION

Although Scar took control of the Pride Lands, he is still jealous of his brother, Mufasa. He is not a good ruler and does not respect the circle of life, so there is no more food left in the Pride Lands. But his reign does not last long; Simba returns to reclaim the throne.

◀5▶

Remember that
the scar runs across
Scar's left eye.

◀6▶

◄**7**►

◄**8**►

SHENZI, BANZAI & ED

This trio of spotted hyenas includes the ringleader Shenzi, the dim troublemaker Banzai, and the speechless but always-laughing Ed. The hyenas are Scar's henchmen, without whom Scar never would have been able to take control of the Pride Lands.

The tallest parts of Shenzi, Banzai, and Ed are their backs, not their heads.

◀2▶

Shenzi has a small "mane" on the top of her head.

◄**3**►

◀4▶

5

◀6▶

Notice Ed's
ears are
notched.

Banzai's eyes are two different shapes—one is slightly narrowed.

◄7►